Joseph

3

C000050574

COLOMBIA
Between the Lines

Photography & Text by

Jason P. Howe

Introduction by Garry M. Leech
Foreword by Jason Burke

First edition published 2008

Images, texts and captions copyright © 2008 Jason P. Howe

Design and Image Post-Production by Andy Higgins
Printed in London, England
Print Managed by Nice Impressions

Introduction text copyright © 2008 Garry M. Leech
Foreword text copyright © 2008 Jason Burke
Author portrait image © 2007 Boaz Zippor

Published by: ConflictPics
26 Eaton Road, Bowdon, Altrincham, Cheshire WA14 3EH, UK
Email: books@ConflictPics.com
Web: www.ConflictPics.com

All rights reserved. No part of this production may be reproduced,
stored in a retrieval system, or transmitted in any form or by any
means, electronic, mechanical, photocopying, recording, or otherwise
without the prior written permission of the author.

ISBN Softback: 978-0-9559125-0-4
ISBN Hardback:978-0-9559125-1-1

The paper used for this publication is produced to Forest Stewardship
Council (FSC) standards, which means wood used to make the
product is from a forest which are well managed according to strict
enviornmental, social and economic standards. The forest of origin
has been independently inspected and evaluated according to
the principles for forest management and approved by the Forest
Stewardship Council. May, 2008.

Dedicated to the people of Colombia and their search for peace

Introduction

The Eternal Conflict By Garry M. Leech

For more than 40 years a civil war has raged in Colombia in which the principal victims have been civilians, particularly those Colombians living in rural regions. Political violence has left more than 200,000 dead and three million people have been forcibly displaced from their homes and land - making Colombia the country with the second-largest internally displaced population in the world after the Sudan. The Colombian people have been caught in the middle of a conflict being waged by the US-backed Colombian military, right-wing paramilitaries and leftist guerrillas that has made the country the worst human rights catastrophe in the Western Hemisphere.

On May 27, 1964, the Colombian military attacked the region of Marquetalia in the department of Tolima. Planes dropped US-supplied bombs on remote villages as 16,000 troops attacked peasants who had settled in the region after fleeing government repression in other areas during the late 1940s and 1950s, a period known as la Violencia.

A small group of armed peasants survived the Marquetalia attack and shortly afterwards formed the Revolutionary Armed Forces of Colombia (FARC). The FARC and the smaller National Liberation Army (ELN), which was also formed in 1964 by middle class intellectuals influenced by the Cuban Revolution, sought to overthrow the government in order to install a socialist regime that would address the country's gross social and economic inequalities.

During the past 40 years of conflict, the FARC and the Colombian government have made several attempts to conduct peace negotiations. In 1985, following the signing of the La Uribe cease-fire accords between the FARC and President Belisario Betancourt, the rebel group established a political party, the Patriotic Union (UP). The Colombian military, however, did not support the peace process. Because it was bound by the cease-fire, the military formed right-wing paramilitary groups to wage a dirty war on its behalf against suspected guerrilla sympathizers. By 1990, paramilitary death squads had assassinated more than 2,000 members of the Patriotic Union, including two presidential candidates and four elected congressmen. Despite the dirty war being waged against the Patriotic Union and numerous cease-fire violations by each side, negotiations continued until the Colombian military launched a surprise attack on the FARC's headquarters at Casa Verde in the department of Meta. Not surprisingly, this blatant violation of the cease-fire ended the peace process.

In 1989, several smaller guerrilla groups - M-19, EPL and Quintín Lame - agreed to demobilize in return for amnesties and a role in the writing of the country's new constitution. The FARC and ELN refused the government's amnesty offer and continued to fight. Some of the demobilized rebels met with the same fate as many Patriotic Union members. Former M-19 commander Carlos Pizarro was assassinated by a paramilitary hit man, while his comrade Antonio Navarro Wolf narrowly survived an attempt on his life. Ultimately, the new constitution failed to improve the economic and social conditions under which the majority of Colombians lived.

In fact, the neo-liberal, or free-market, economic program that the government was launching at that time was a non-negotiable issue in the debate to formulate the new constitution.

While the FARC's political wing had been devastated by the dirty war waged against it, the rebel group's military fronts remained intact. The group continued its war against the government throughout the 1990s, while repeatedly criticizing the neo-liberal economic reforms that were partly responsible for 64 percent of Colombians living in poverty by the end of the decade. Also at this time, US counter-narcotics strategies in Peru and Bolivia caused coca cultivation to shift to FARC-controlled areas in southern Colombia. By taxing coca growers and traffickers that operated in its territory, the rebel group's revenues increased dramatically - supplementing its income from kidnapping and extortion - enabling it to grow to a force of 18,000 fighters.

Many of the paramilitary groups formed in the 1980s by the Colombian military, drug traffickers and wealthy landowners also increased in strength due to proceeds from the drug trade. By the time the various paramilitary groups were incorporated into one umbrella organization called the United Self-Defence Forces of Colombia (AUC) in 1997, they constituted a force of 12,000 fighters. According to human rights groups, the paramilitaries were responsible for more than 70 percent of the country's human rights abuses during the 1990s.

In 1998, President Andrés Pastrana was elected on a peace platform and shortly after assuming office he withdrew 2,000 soldiers and police from a Switzerland-sized area of territory in Caquetá and Meta. Pastrana turned the demilitarised zone over to the FARC, who agreed to hold peace talks with the government in its new 'safe-haven.' Unlike the 1980s talks, however, there would be no cease-fire during these negotiations; the war would continue outside of the demilitarised zone.

Government and rebel negotiators agreed to a 12-point agenda that included discussing economic and social restructuring, agrarian reform, the exploitation of the country's natural resources, the human rights situation and military reform. The state of the country's economy was the first topic addressed.

After three years of negotiations, however, negotiators had failed to move beyond the initial topic, primarily because the US-pushed neo-liberal globalisation process was still non-negotiable as far as Bogotá and Washington were concerned.

On 20 February 2002, sensing growing public frustration with the oft-stalled negotiations and following the FARC's kidnapping of Colombian Senator Jorge Gechem Turbay, President Pastrana ended the fledgling three-year peace process. Pastrana used the FARC's ongoing military operations and 'terrorist' activities during negotiations as justification for ordering the Colombian military's invasion of the rebel safe-haven. But while the FARC was condemned for continuing to wage war outside the rebel zone, few questioned the fact that the Colombian military and the paramilitaries were doing exactly the same thing.

During negotiations, the FARC had repeatedly stated that it would not agree to a cease-fire until the government dismantled the paramilitaries. One of the most ignored facts related to the peace process's failure was the tragic legacy of the 1980's cease-fire accord that led to the decimation of the Patriotic Union. The FARC was not about to make the same mistake again.

Under President Pastrana, the so-called 'peace candidate,' not only were the paramilitaries not dismantled, they actually experienced their greatest growth and military successes. The Colombian military also strengthened itself under the Pastrana administration due to the Colombian president's success in obtaining more than $1 billion in US counter-narcotics aid under Plan Colombia, a programme which primarily targeted coca-growing peasants and the FARC.

Following 9/11, the Bush administration convinced the US Congress to lift conditions restricting the use of US military aid to counter-narcotics operations. As a result, Plan Colombia funding and other US military aid could be used to fight a counterinsurgency war against the FARC as part of the global war on terror. The FARC responded to new offensives launched by the Colombian military by breaking up into smaller units and returning to traditional hit-and-run guerrilla tactics.

Meanwhile, in July 2003, newly elected President Alvaro Uribe announced an agreement to begin talks with the AUC intended to lead to a demobilization of the paramilitaries. This decision came six months after AUC leaders Carlos Castaño and Salvatore Mancuso had announced a unilateral cease-fire with the government - although in reality the paramilitaries and the Colombian Army rarely fought against each other. However, the cease-fire soon proved to be a charade as paramilitaries killed more than 1,800 unarmed civilians over the next 20 months.

The Bush administration's endorsement of the paramilitary peace negotiations stood in sharp contrast to Washington's blatant lack of support for President Pastrana's failed peace talks with the FARC.

Washington refused to actively support the Pastrana peace process unless the FARC first handed over the rebels responsible for killing three US human rights activists in 1999. The Bush administration, however, chose to actively support the paramilitary peace process without demanding that Castaño and Mancuso turn themselves over to authorities for extradition on warrants issued by US courts.

Under a controversial Justice and Peace Law passed by the Colombian Congress in June 2005, most demobilized paramilitary leaders could spend as little as 22 months in jail even if they had perpetrated crimes against humanity. The law also lacked enforcement mechanisms to ensure that demobilized paramilitary leaders dismantled their criminal, particularly drug trafficking, networks.

Ultimately, the demobilization process proved to be more of a restructuring as many demobilized paramilitaries continued to wage their dirty war against those Colombians struggling for social justice, including unionists, human rights defenders, and peasant and indigenous leaders.

After more than 40 years, the Colombian conflict continues to rage with the military, paramilitaries and guerrillas targeting the civilian population. Every year, thousands of Colombians are killed or 'disappeared,' while hundreds of thousands more are forcibly displaced from their homes and land.

In 2005, the United Nations listed the Colombian conflict as one of the world's most under-reported humanitarian crises.

During my many years of covering Colombia's conflict, I was lucky to have the opportunity to work with British photojournalist Jason Howe. Jason has exhibited a true desire to capture all aspects of the Colombian tragedy in order to shed light on this 'under-reported humanitarian crisis.' His lens has captured the anguish of those who have lost loved ones, the desperation of those who have been forcibly displaced, and the lives of combatants on all sides. At times, Jason's commitment has brought him a little too close to the subject matter.

In Caquetá, he snapped images of terrified civilians caught in the midst of a firefight between the Colombian Army and FARC guerrillas. And in Saravena, the two of us found ourselves in the town's darkened streets surrounded by gunfire during a prolonged night time battle between rebels and the Colombian National Police.

Thanks to Jason's dedication, however, people throughout the world can now catch a unique and powerful glimpse of Colombia's seemingly endless human tragedy. Hopefully, this book will increase global awareness of the plight endured by millions of Colombians and contribute to the achievement of a just and lasting peace.

Garry Leech is an independent journalist and editor of Colombia Journal (www.colombiajournal.org). He is the author of Crude Interventions: The United States, Oil and the New World (Dis) Order (Zed Books, 2006) and Killing Peace: Colombia's Conflict and the Failure of US Intervention (Inota, 2002), and co-author of The People Behind Colombian Coal: Mining, Multinationals and Human Rights (Pisando Callos, 2007). His articles have appeared in various publications in the United States, Canada, Europe, Australia and Latin America.

Foreword

By Jason Burke

It was a long way from the jungles, the high, cloud-wreathed hills, the grey, stinking shanty towns of Colombia's cities. It was a searing hot day in the dustbowl of central Iraq. A small group of Western journalists stand amid the narrow alleys and the cemeteries of Najaf, one of the holiest sites in Islam.

It is three o'clock in the afternoon and the bright sunlight is blasting all colour out of the cloudless sky. Milling groups of young fighters, all militants with the Mahdi Army, one of the militias that have sprung up in post-Saddam Iraq, viscerally anti-Western, unpredictable and often violent, lean listlessly against the walls. And in the middle of it a photographer, bearded, in desert boots, a stream of good-natured expletives directed at friends and enemies alike and a broad gap-toothed smile, equally promiscuous, is working hard.

It was the first time I had run across Jason Howe. Over the next few weeks and over the next year or so in Iraq we would work side by side on many occasions. And, as the situation got steadily worse and our days became increasingly restricted to the city limits of Baghdad and then to certain areas within the city itself and then, almost, just the hotels, I got to know Jason and his work better. All that I learned confirmed that first impression on the streets of Najaf in the summer of 2003 and is confirmed by the photos and the faces and the events that make up this book.

There are several ways of telling a story. The best is from the bottom up.

You can interview ministers, attend scores of press conferences, read scores of cuttings or books. But nothing beats lived experience on the ground. There is an old saying about war: 'the closer you get, the less you know.' Which is true, in the sense that rarely does anyone in the middle of any fighting actually see the big picture. But they do see the small picture – and that is often far more revealing.

Watching Jason at work in Iraq I understood a little about the strange journey that had led him from a home in eastern England through Latin America and on to the badlands of Iraq.

Jason did not study photography or journalism. He considered, he told me once, signing up for a course but decided in the end that it would be better to just go and get stuck in and learn as he went along. He set off to Colombia with a Leica and 50 rolls of film. Within a few months he had lived in a FARC rebel camp, been in his first fire fight, narrowly missed getting blown to bits by a booby trap bomb that killed several of the soldiers he was with and met coca farmers, drug dealers, paramilitaries and the girl who he later became romantically involved with and who turned out to be an assassin.

The images – those of the female killer and her child are some of the saddest of the book - won an award and were the basis of Jason being invited to join the agency that encouraged him to travel out to Iraq where he arrived just a few days before the capture of Saddam. He went on to spend more than 14 months reporting from Iraq.

What stands out among these pictures is the view of the photographer. Not only is Jason close, but he is low down. He is with the people he is photographing. He is sometimes far closer, you could argue, far closer emotionally as well as physically, than a journalist should be. But this brings an immediacy and a vibrancy to the images that lacks so often.

There is also modesty here, a surprising humility for those who know Jason at his bombastic best (or worst). The best writers trust their material. They take themselves out of what they write, allowing their subject matter to speak for them. This is what this photographer does.

In a world increasingly dominated by reporters who make themselves the centre of the story, particularly those reporters who work with images, images that genuinely reveal something about somewhere and someone, without lecturing the viewer, without vaunting the courage and intelligence of the journalist, without making grandiose claims about the motives of the reporter, are a rarity. And all the more valuable for it.

Jason Burke is Chief Correspondent for the Observer newspaper. He is the author of On the Road to Kandahar, (Allen Lane 2006) and Al-Qaeda: The True Story of Radical Islam, (Penguin Books Ltd, 2004).

Following Page:
A US trained anti narcotics policemen provides security at a helicopter landing zone whilst on operations in the Sierra Nevada Mountains.

Farclandia

6th November

San Vicente del Caguan - The peace talks have been suspended. The FARC are breaking up their camps and melting back into the jungle.

I waited for three hours at a military checkpoint on the edge of the zone. It took a lot of arguing but eventually they let me pass. After a night in San Vicente I headed out for the rebels' political base. Unless the talks resume the FARC will not give access to any journalist.

On arrival I saw two commanders I had met on my first visit. They remembered me from last year and loved the prints I brought. With their approval, I'm now living in a disused camp, sleeping under my mozzie net. I walk to a nearby town to buy food; I endure the wait. So far it has been only three days. I might have to wait just one more day for a change in the situation, maybe several weeks. It's not a problem: I've come so far and waited so long for my permit. I need to acclimatize to this vicious heat and humidity so I am running circuits of the camp, trying to get fit for any jungle incursions.

It's tense around here. People really have no idea what the future holds. If the FARC pulls out, who will take over? Maybe the military? If so, the people will probably be safe. But what if it's the paramilitaries? Then anyone who helped the FARC in any way could be killed. Anyway, no dramas right now.

Hopefully my patience will pay off and I will spend some quality time in a big camp. After that, who knows?

22nd November

So, after two weeks in rebel-controlled territory what have I managed to get done? A lot of waiting mainly. I was with Paul, an Australian traveller and Elena, another photographer. They both complained of boredom on an hourly basis and constantly wound each other up. It was amusing for about a day.

I enjoyed the chance to soak up some sun, do a bit of running and just acclimatize. The heat, humidity and voracious insects made it tough at times.

After a week, Paul gave up and headed back to Bogotá. The zone was not really as he had expected; he imagined it would be swarming with rebels, but in reality you have to seek them out. Like me, he expected to witness some combat, but had not realized that first we would have to exit the safe zone, where there is no fighting. Elena had been here before and so knew what to expect, but two days after Paul she quit too.

The reason we weren't allowed to visit the camps was security. The FARC is on a war footing and many big camps have been broken up, with the fighters hiding in small groups to lessen the threat of bombing by Government forces. The FARC obviously doesn't want anyone to know where their troops are at the moment. However, they allowed me to shoot pictures at their roadblocks. I got images of them stopping and searching the civilians. At a camp I photographed the guerrillas playing football, washing clothes, butchering a pig, chopping firewood, cooking, learning radio craft and other day-to-day stuff.

Today I made pictures of a young couple I knew from my last visit - now boyfriend and girlfriend. I loved the contrast between their happy carefree expressions and their serious attire and weapons.

27th November

Bringing the photos I took last time was the best thing possible -they have been my passport to success with everyone. One commander promised to get in contact when it is possible to make similar images, with hundreds of rebels instead of a handful. When I explain that I gave up my home and job to come and tell their story, entirely at my own expense, it does gain me some respect, as does asking to put myself into the same situations they expose themselves to.

I am now in San Vicente, which is incredibly similar to Woodbridge, my home town, and I love it here. The people are very friendly. I have found a place to stay for $2.50 per night and the eating here is good and cheap. I can imagine living here. It's hot, sunny, with a nice river, beautiful chicas and an increasingly volatile situation.
What more could I ask for?

Unless anything dramatic happens in the next 36 hours, I will leave San Vicente by river and head for Cartagena - not the famous city, but a village along the Rio Caguan. From there I will leave the protection of the FARC and their safe zone and move into disputed regions on my way by river to Puerto Leguizimo and the military base there, to ask if I can accompany them on their patrols of the region.

Before leaving the zone I am sending all FARC-related photos and documents back to Bogotá to lessen the chances of trouble if searched by paramilitaries. My exposed film is going back by plane with a Kiwi I met in San Vicente. I found out that the taxi driver who was killed recently was the guy I used last time. Some paramilitaries posing as journalists hired him to take them to a fairly remote point, then shot him in the mouth. I need to be really careful what I say and to whom from now on, especially as the paras sometimes use FARC uniforms at their roadblocks to trick people.

From here on it gets more and more difficult to know who, if anyone, to trust.

Puerto Rico - This morning I ventured out of the rebel enclave to this small town. It's only about an hour beyond the last FARC checkpoint, but it's in a different world. This is where the taxi driver was killed. The streets here swarm with heavily armed military and police, holding their weapons at the ready and searching-out insurgents. Photographing them was extremely difficult. They fear the rebels will take my film and use the images to target them.

During the night the paramilitaries assassinated two men in Puerto Rico. I noticed the lines of fresh graves in the local cemetery. The dates on the nearest crosses were all from this month. This was a relatively hot zone. Bodies turned up every few days. The FARC, military and paras all fought within the confines of this small town.

At one side of the cemetery lay a coffin with its lid already nailed shut. Finding the other body was a matter of tracing the awful smell and the buzzing sound. I stood on a pile of bricks and peered into a nearby building. It was very dark but I could make out a naked body lying on the morgue gurney. On the table, bloated and fly-covered, lay the remains of a man who had been walking the streets of this town the day before. The flies busily went about their work, undisturbed by my intrusion. The man had been shot in the face, removing a large portion of it. What was left had been burnt; or perhaps that was done before he was shot. Also, it appeared that someone had tried to cut off one of his legs. The body had already swollen to twice its normal size in the heat and the stench was overpowering. It was my first close-up glimpse of the cost of this conflict.

I decided not to stay overnight in Puerto Rico. By mid-afternoon the military had left the streets, leaving them clear for others to go about their dirty work. There were too many people asking too many questions. I returned to San Vicente to pack up my stuff. I have received news that all the films I shot last week have arrived safely back in Bogotá. Tomorrow I head upriver.

Marie Sol, a FARC recruit patrols the perimeter
of a camp near San Vicente del Caguan.

A female FARC recruit in front of a billboard criticizing 'Plan Colombia' and US intervention in Colombia. San Vicente del Caguan.

Following page: A FARC rebel with his mascot, a wildcat at a checkpoint. Caquetá.

A FARC rebel chats with a young passenger at a checkpoint.
Caquetá.

A young boy watches as a bus load of passengers are searched for weapons by a FARC rebel at a checkpoint.
Caquetá.

A group of FARC recruits clean their camp near San Vicente del Caguan.

Preparing a pig for the camp kitchen. Caquetá.

« Training on an assault course in a FARC camp near San Vicente del Caguan.

A female rebel applies her make up in preparation for a party in her camp near San Vicente del Caguan.

Male and female rebels share an open air shower in their camp in Caquetá. »

FARC recruits, Marie Sol and Bernardo, kiss whilst on an evening stroll near their camp. Caquetá.

Coca

7th December

Puerto Asís - I got as far as Penas Colorado before my time and money started running low.

At Cartagena del Chaira I waited 24 hours for a boat to Penas Colorado. These towns were getting progressively duller, full of cowboys and whores, neither group particularly photogenic. The price of everything rose with every river mile I travelled.

In Penas I hit a small FARC patrol and was told that without authorization I could go no further, or even leave town for that matter. I already had permission from the commanders, but once out of their patch their power had diminished quickly, leaving me to fend for myself.

Penas was not even a one-horse town. I realized I could very easily get stuck further up-river with no money and no way of getting any sent to me. So I decided to skip town, back the way I came. I hopped on the next boat to Puerto Rico, then by road to San Vicente. My friend in Bogotá wired me some cash so I could move on.

In San Vicente the night before, I met a French woman working with the Red Cross and arranged to go out partying with her and her friends in Florencia, if I got that far. I ended up spending all my time talking, drinking and dancing with locals. I stumbled to bed at six a.m.

I woke up feeling demoralised. I have been out in the sticks now for four weeks. There have been too many delays and failures. I have no one to discuss things with. I haven't spoken English for two or three weeks and in that time have shot very few photos. It's a huge amount of time invested for relatively little in return.

I decided to press on towards the Putumayo, one of the narco trafficking centers of Colombia. It took a couple of days to get from Florencia to Puerto Asís, the capital of the department. En-route I began talking with a beautiful Colombian girl called Marylin who invited me to stay with her family; they have a small roadside store and bar on the outskirts of town. I explained my purpose in visiting the region and Marylin told me she had friends in both the paramilitaries and the military, so would be able to help. I was very attracted to Marylin but had no idea how close we would become and how the future between us would unfold.

I talked my way into the nearby military camp and asked the commander to take me out on some operations in the area. Unfortunately, all permission for this has to come from Bogotá, so no chance here and now. So I asked him if he knew where I could locate the guys growing and processing the coca. I thought it worth a try, and it worked. He patiently explained where the nearest plantation was, telling me the Military had destroyed it previously, but it had all been replanted.

I set off with an hour or so of good light left. I asked many people along the road who pointed this way and that. Eventually a man offered to lead me to the plantation. I followed him across the fields and there, in the dying light, was my first view of Colombia's most infamous plant.

As I began to trudge home I met another man who said he too had some coca. He invited me to sit with him while his wife brought a glass of hot milk. As we sat he explained how the war-on-drugs affected the local people. How the government had promised them money if they destroyed their crops, but then refused later to pay, leaving the people with no crops and no money.

I asked if he would take me to his plantation and he agreed to meet me next morning at first light. He led me through a flooded forest, ankle-deep in mud, to his plantation. It actually belonged to a co-operative of 18 families and covered 25 hectares. The farmer told me that the coca would be ready to harvest in one month. The problem is the workers are scared to be photographed alongside these illegal crops.

Both the FARC and the Paras have middlemen buying the coca paste for them to have processed in factories that they control. The main danger faced by the farmers is not from the military and its war on drugs, but the groups competing to buy their crop. If they sell it to the FARC´s buyer then the Paras will be after them and vice versa; pretty much a no-win situation. But because the demand for and income from this crop far exceeds anything else they could possibly grow, then really the farmers have little choice but to grow coca - not if they want to keep feeding their families and sending their kids to school.

Tomorrow I am moving on to a small village called El Tigre. It is supposedly a paramilitary stronghold, as are the next few villages on my route. I hope to meet with the paras and see if they will take me to a cocaine factory. I also want to see if the death squads are hard at work in these towns. First stop: the cemetery.

Coca leaves, Putumayo.

A mother and daughter set off from their farm to the coca fields.
Putumayo.

Harvesting coca on a cooperative plantation on the bank of Rio Putumayo.

Harvesting coca near Puerto Asís, Putumayo.

Young people working with alternative crops.
Putumayo.

A young boy carrying machetes runs for cover during a tropical downpour.
Putumayo.

A coca farmer adds lime to coca leaves before soaking them in kerosene as part of the process to extract the alkaloid that is used to make cocaine. Putumayo.

1kg of coca paste requires the picking and processing of more than 550 kilos of coca leaf.
Putumayo.

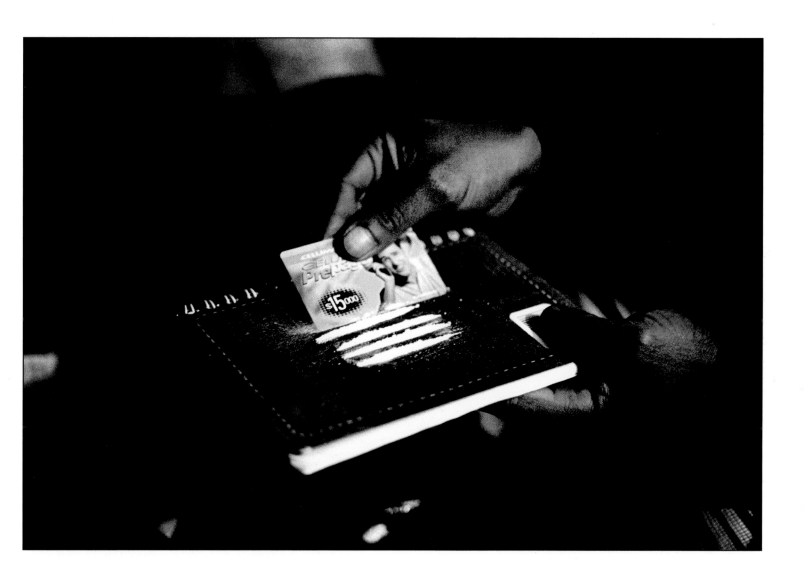

The final product, cocaine hydrochloride is cut into lines by a dealer.
Bogotá.

Los Posos

10th January

Los Posos - I arrived back in the rebel zone on New Years Eve and headed out to the camp at Los Posos, hoping to photograph the celebrations. The commander said I was welcome to join the party and I could stay for a few days if I wanted. Perfect! The camp had luckily grown in numbers to about 30 fighters plus visitors for the party. I got some good shots, but unfortunately the rebels got me so drunk that I passed out before the New Year arrived.

The next few days produced some good images. The rebels are now used to me photographing them eating, sleeping, showering and going about every aspect of daily life. One or two have asked me not to shoot them, so I don't, but the rest have no problem.

The other day I had to leave the camp at 7 a.m. to go to a city outside the zone to extend my visa. I arrived there around midday and had to wait until 2 p.m. for the office to open. It became a race against time to get the visa and find transport back into the zone. Once 6 p.m. comes no one wants to be caught out on the road. I found a driver who agreed to take me for a hefty price. We barely dropped below 120 km/h, on roads where really 80 was pushing the limits of safe travel. Once or twice we hit 140; windows down, no seat-belts, music blasting - fantastic fun! At every checkpoint we were told we could not go on, but somehow I blagged my way through and we arrived in San Vicente just after dark.

I found a truck full of cattle heading towards the camp. I stood in the back in the dark for over an hour, trying not to get crushed by cows as we bumped over the dirt roads. I also avoided getting shot by the camp's sentry and, although everyone had turned-in, there in the kitchen was a mess tin with my dinner. After a gruelling day this thoughtfulness meant a hell of lot.

Bad news: As of yesterday afternoon the 3-year-old peace process here in Colombia has been abandoned. Neither the FARC nor the Government has agreed to the demands of the other side, or compromised in any way, and therefore both groups left the purpose built site near San Vicente and the negotiating table for possibly the last time. At a very tense press conference both sides read statements before speeding away in different directions geographically, but in reality, both heading towards all-out war.

The Government has given the FARC 48 hours to evacuate the 42,000 square kilometer zone before the military tries to retake it. The Government has sworn to respect the rights of civilians living in towns within the zone, but no such statement or action is likely from the paramilitaries who are eager to wipe out those suspected of collaborating with the rebels. Other correspondents tell me there are already paras living secretly within San Vicente waiting to begin their death-squad activities.

Several journalists are preparing to leave before the shit hits the fan. I plan to wait for the 48 hour deadline to expire and see if the Government does in fact send in the troops. Already the TV screens in the bars and brothels all over town are full of images of tanks, helicopters and truckloads of troops, heading towards the zone to back up those already surrounding us.

The locals say that if the military tries to retake San Vicente then everyone here will fight like rebels. But will they really?

FARC rebels dance at a New Year celebration in their camp. Caquetá.

Negotiations

22nd January

San Vicente del Caguan - Colombia has just passed through the most tense crisis of the peace process - troops massed around the FARC zone awaiting orders from the President to invade and retake control. Various deadlines were set. It appeared as though the search for a peaceful solution was over and full-scale war inevitable. The UN's special envoy tried a last-ditch attempt to hold things together. Just four hours before deadline he managed to get the FARC to back-down on a sufficient number of issues to stall the invasion. The Government allowed the FARC another few days to come up with a plan for peace.

As the High Commissioner for Peace and Ambassadors from around the world rejoined the FARC at the negotiating table, the journalists and photographers searched their faces for signs of how things were going. There was a lot of tension. If the military did come to town so would the paramilitaries and with them the torture, or assassination, of all suspects having links with the FARC. This would include people we knew in the town.

The townsfolk of San Vicente and other settlements marched on the peace talks. The children had peace slogans written on their faces. Everyone, young or old, was waving either a Colombian flag or a white flag of peace, their very presence imploring the International Envoys to help the Government and FARC find a solution to this crisis. Many were, in reality, begging for their lives.

Last night an agreement was reached. The rebels would be allowed to keep their zone if they stuck to a timetable of demands set by the Government leading towards a ceasefire from the 10th of April.

The crisis had passed and the search for peace continues. In the meantime the FARC continue to display their military power. Every day they blow up bridges or set off car bombs in towns up and down the country killing many civilians and they are also kidnapping more and more.

The view that they are the good guys in this conflict faded in my mind some time ago, sadly they seem as bad as everyone else. Certainly the foot soldiers I lived with I liked and they became friends. Many joined the FARC because for them it was the best, or in some cases, the only option. However the men who control and manipulate their young and desperate minds into becoming killing machines I find it hard to feel any respect for.

Undoubtedly, many of them have valid reasons for their desire to make war, but for many the quest for power is the strongest motivation, nothing more nothing less.
 In the end it seems there are no good guys.

I am leaving this afternoon to begin the lengthy journey back down to Putumayo to attempt to make contact with the paramilitaries in the hamlet of El Tigre.

Local villagers converge on peace talks between the FARC and a team of Government negotiators. Los Posos, Caquetá.

6th February

La Hormiga - Meeting the paramilitaries went smoothly enough. It was rather tense to begin with. I received conflicting advice on who was actually in control in El Tigre. Some locals told me the rebels were but the military told me the paras had control. I approached the town with some trepidation as it wasn't certain who I would meet.

The paras took some hunting down as they keep a fairly low profile. Eventually I came across a couple of heavy-looking guys sitting outside a house in a back street. Something told me these were the guys to talk to. I asked them if they knew where I should look for authorization to work in the town.

Under their shirts they had hand-guns tucked in their waist-bands. This told me I was already in the right place. They took me to meet their commander, where I explained my project. He informed me that he was head of the local self defence force, known to everyone else as paras. He was polite and helpful and took me for a drive around the town so that everyone would know he had OK'd me.

Later, over beers, I asked if he could get me into a para camp and he said at present it was impossible but maybe in the future. I was disappointed but had at least made that initial contact which is always the hardest. I got access to some massive coca plantations and permission to photograph the campasinos working there.

19th February

Puerto Asís - I'm feeling rather jaded and pissed off and can't wait to get out of here! I'm really looking forward to getting home to see everyone again but am worried that I haven't achieved enough and will regret leaving here.

My money has run out, I'm very tired and generally in a bad frame of mind. It's probably more sensible to finish up the pictures I need to do here and then get going. My negative outlook brightens whenever I go out and the light is nice and I get some good work done but it keeps coming back. That probably means it's time for a rest. I need to learn some lessons from this trip and not make the same time and money wasting mistakes again.

If I can get both my head and the funds together I will hold on a bit longer.

Young girls with Paz (peace in Spanish) painted on their faces wave flags during negotiations between the Government and the FARC. Los Posos, Caquetá.

Bus Bomb

28th February

Florencia - I sped along the deserted roads of southern Colombia's savannah, crammed into a taxi with two French photographers and a Spanish writer. In the back we chain-smoked Piel Roja cigarettes, the local brand, while up front Salud the writer put her one and only tape on the car stereo: ABBA's greatest hits.

We were making a dash from San Vicente del Caguan to Florencia. San Vicente had been the capital of the rebel-controlled demilitarised zone until a few days before. A three-year search for peace had skidded to an inglorious halt when the FARC rebels hijacked a domestic flight. The president ordered his troops to start retaking the rebel zone. Before withdrawing, the rebels had destroyed the local power and communication systems. Here and there a petrol generator could be found and a few journalists used sat-phones. But most of us needed to reach an unaffected town to file our stories, wire our pictures and find a working ATM.

I clambered into the cab with little hesitation when Salud told me where they were heading. Bleary-eyed and dozy after a late night at a local bar, we had travelled a few kilometres before I realised how unprepared I was for this little jaunt. The roads ahead were reportedly impassable due to rebel roadblocks. I had only a few rolls of film in my bag and, for the first time in five months, I was moving through a combat zone without a bullet-proof vest.

We passed through several roadblocks, some manned by young rebel fighters keen to show a brave face despite enduring hundreds of bombing missions flown over the previous nights. Other roadblocks were run by government troops. At each one we climbed out and showed our press cards, took a few photos, and got on our way again.

A few days before the motorcade of presidential candidate Ingrid Bettencourt had been stopped at a roadblock made up of two buses and a truck. We approached the remains of the roadblock where the FARC kidnapped her and torched the cars. Our driver stopped some distance away and we approached on foot. We photographed the burnt-out cars and torn signs her supporters had abandoned. One bus had a misspelt message painted on its side, warning that the bus should not be moved because it was booby trapped with explosives.

The locals were more accustomed to blocked highways and quickly created a gap wide enough for our driver to squeeze his cab through. We were on our way again. A few bends later we came across a large group of soldiers walking back towards the roadblock where they told us their bomb squad would clear the way.

As the only person in the taxi with no deadline or pressing need to get to Florencia, I decided to return with the soldiers to photograph them blowing up the bus. The soldiers were initially a little cool and answered questions without any chit-chat. The captain told me to keep my distance, but I argued that it would be impossible to get a decent shot from hundreds of metres away. I naively thought I was a good judge of what was a safe distance. When the captain's attention was elsewhere, I slipped off with some troops to examine the bus. It was a slow process. A few homemade mines were found and removed. The soldiers warmed up a bit: we shared cigarettes and they seemed happy with my presence.

They attached a hook and line to the handles of the bus's cargo doors, then jerked the doors open. Sometimes I was shooting pictures only a metre or so behind them. As I followed them around to the other side of the bus, one soldier waved me back. Annoyed, I wandered off behind the other disabled bus, perhaps 10 or 15 metres away. I glanced down at my Leica to check how much film I had left.

The explosion ripped through the bus the soldiers were searching. I felt shards of metal slam into the bus I stood behind. Shattered glass showered the road. The blast made me stagger. My ears were ringing, and it took a moment for me to catch my breath, for my brain to register what had happened.

I heard a soldier calling out to his colleagues. He got no response. I waded through the smoke and debris littering the road, pausing to take a picture, then rounded the destroyed bus. What I saw was brutal. The soldiers I had spent the afternoon with lay dead or wounded on the tarmac. Stunned by the carnage, my heart raced and my hands shook uncontrollably. I tried to adjust the settings on my cameras. I knew what I should be doing, but taking those next few steps toward the shattered and smoking bodies required a lot of will-power. Instinctively I glanced around, but today I was alone. There was no pack of combat-hardened photojournalists to show me how to behave.

How far away were the rebels who planted this bomb? Were they watching? Had they set it off? Was there another timed to explode when more soldiers arrived or would the rebels now attack? I had stuck my head too far into a lion's mouth and wondered if I had time to pull it out before those jaws snapped shut and it was all over. I took a deep breath and moved forward.

The first soldier had been blown off the road. His skin was scorched and peeling, his clothes in shreds. One arm had been ripped off at the elbow. He was beyond help. The other two soldiers lay in a tangle in the middle of the road. One had been torn open from throat to groin, spilling his insides over the tarmac. Bright red blood trailed away from his corpse. One arm was missing and his other limbs lay twisted at impossible angles.

The body on top groaned and moved slightly. Incredibly, one soldier had survived, perhaps shielded from the worst of the blast by his friend's body. The explosion had shattered his legs and peppered them with flying shrapnel. He was still clutching his friend's dead body, as if it would protect him from further harm. His eyes flicked between the gutted bus and his dead colleague, then back again, as if he couldn't comprehend what had happened. Then his pain-filled eyes met mine.

My brain was screaming with conflicting emotions. I felt a mixture of guilt and excitement at being presented with this extreme subject matter. If I could just hold it together it would make powerful pictures. "Sorry," I mouthed to the soldier, and started to shoot.

A breathless young medic arrived, looking confused and equally unprepared for this situation. His hard-faced companion took his medical bag and began treating the soldier. All around me were shocked and angry faces as the soldiers saw what had happened to their friends. I made a few more shots and then took a much needed cigarette break.

The dead bodies were carried to a landing zone while the wounded soldier was prepared for evacuation. Two helicopter gunships clattered through the fading light, swooping overhead as the medivac chopper touched down. The stretcher was quickly loaded. As the helicopter pulled sharply away the wounded soldier, through a haze of morphine, was still weeping for his dead friends and his own shattered legs.

Evacuating the dead was left for a safer day.

A wounded Government soldier lies on top of his dead companion moments after an explosion. FARC rebels planted a bomb in a bus thereby blocking a main highway to facilitate a kidnapping and disrupt transportation and commerce in the area. El Paujil, Caquetá.

Government soldiers treat their wounded colleague minutes after two other soldiers were killed by a FARC booby trap. El Paujil, Caquetá.

Government soldiers treat and evacuate a wounded companion from the scene of a rebel bomb attack.
El Paujil, Caquetá.

Firefight

10th March

San Vicente - Things are really hotting up down here. The rebels no longer have the freedom of the safe zone since the peace process fell apart and are on the offensive. They are setting up roadblocks every day and waiting for the army to deploy and engage them.

I left town yesterday afternoon along with two other photographer friends, Eros and Hector, and a car full of TV and print journos. After a few kilometers of empty roads we stopped to assess the situation. The print and TV guys decided to turn back, it looked as though there could be some fighting ahead and the road could be blocked. They were worried that if we went too far we may get cut off and be unable to return to San Vicente. Hector, Eros and I were keen to push on. If there was some fighting up the highway then it seemed the logical place to be. We drove on until we reached a line of trucks and cars stopped in the road. The FARC had set up a roadblock and had 40 or 50 civilians sitting on the ground next to their vehicles.

We parked up and began walking along the grass verge to where we could see the FARC fighters crouching in a ditch. Before we got to them the crack of high velocity rounds passing overhead had us belly down in the ditch. I scuttled back to the car to retrieve my bullet proof vest, at last feeling that dragging it around for weeks had been worth it. When we reached their position I spotted a young female FARC rebel who I had photographed at a checkpoint a few weeks ago. I asked her if it was OK for us to work, she shrugged and nodded.

More shots rang out. It was hard to tell from what direction the shooting was coming with the nearby mountains creating strange acoustics. The civilians were cowering beneath their cars shrieking with fear at each new burst of gunfire.

The rebels were effectively using the civilians as a human shield. They hunkered down in the ditch with the people and vehicles between them and the Government soldiers who were wading across the river firing as they came.

The rebels began to spread out a bit. A couple of them moved into the fields beside the road and knelt or stood up just long enough to fire a burst from their Kalashnikovs then disappeared back into the long grass. We couldn't yet see the soldiers but they were still firing in our direction though with some caution I imagine given all the civilians in the road. When they got closer the rebels decided it was time to bug out.

As the gunfire slackened the people trapped on the road made a dash for safety. Petrified looking men and women, some carrying babies crawled under a barbed wire fence and into a ditch and surrounding swamp. Eros and Hector had been concentrating on photographing these people waving their white flags fashioned out of shirts and towels ran with them. I decided to stay with the rebels for a while longer, but as they withdrew I was left stranded on the wrong side of the road.

The soldiers were getting very close, everyone else was in the grass keeping their heads down and I was alone in what had been the rebel position until moments before.

Hector and Eros say that as I crossed the road they could see bullets striking the ground around me. Only when I saw the dirt and grass kicking up very close by and felt the crack of rounds passing close overhead did I hit the ground and scrambled under the fence. When I dropped to the ground they thought I had been hit and looked pretty relieved when I crawled through the grass towards them with a big grin on my face.

We were photographing the people crouching in the undergrowth as the troops came through. Suddenly the return fire from the rebels lessened and everyone ran for it. The trucks, taxis and cars all took off in the direction of the river. The bridge had been destroyed by the rebels during the night so the vehicles had to struggle across the river. Our battered old taxi was never going to make it so we pulled over at a safe location. Once we had regained our breath we drove slowly back past the site of the firefight and on to San Vicente.

We were all grinning like lunatics and talking non-stop. It was the first time any of us had witnessed any kind of combat firsthand and we were buzzing from the intensity of the experience. I didn't know how strong the images would be and felt I had not shot that much. I had found checking exposure, focusing and changing films on the Leica all pretty hard to do under fire but it was the first time. Hopefully next time it will be easier.

Our car was stopped at a FARC checkpoint near to town. The rebels peered suspiciously at our ripped and mud smeared clothes but let us pass. They told us that they would be burning vehicles that used this road the next day. We asked if that would include ours or whether we could come out and get some pictures, the rebels said that wouldn't be a problem. That did not turn out to be the case. We headed out again next morning but when we hit the first group rebels they told us to get out of the car and then confiscated it. The surly fighters held us for six or more hours. Later they moved us off of the strip of tarmac and into the trees beside the road.

I tried to relieve the unpleasant situation by telling some jokes. The rebels looked rather confused as we sat clutching our bellies with laughter.

When I told my favourite joke the curious looks on their faces became too much so Hector translated the joke into Spanish for them. By the time they had finished laughing the mood was considerably less tense. They even got us some drinks and snacks from a nearby village. As daylight faded we were sent on our way with a warning never to venture this way again.

All in all I am very satisfied with this trip. I've been given a taste of the reality of working in a war-zone and witnessed combat. The key now is not to push my luck too far.

A woman carrying her baby runs for cover during a brief lull in a firefight between FARC rebels and Government troops. Puerto Rico, Caquetá.

A female FARC fighter crouches in a ditch as Government troops fire on her position.
Puerto Rico, Caquetá.

Civilians seek cover in a roadside ditch whilst caught in crossfire. FARC rebels had been holding them hostage to provoke a rescue attempt from the troops based nearby. Puerto Rico, Caquetá.

Counter Insurgency troops cross a river in pursuit of FARC fighters after the rebels destroyed a bridge and held civilians hostage. Puerto Rico, Caquetá.

Arauca

7th February

Saravena - Garry Leech and I arrived here on Monday morning and got straight to work. We met with both the military and the local police. They operate from a fortified building flanked by ruins - the result of home-made mortar bombs the FARC had pounded them with on more than 60 occasions last year. This is one of the most attacked towns in Colombia.

Over the last few days we have been out on foot-patrols with squads of police through rebel-controlled barrios. The patrols consist of fifteen heavily armed policemen wearing body-armour and Kevlar helmets.

We also enjoyed great access to the military base where I photographed daily life, training and got to speak with the US Special Forces personnel. We were strictly forbidden to photograph them so I had to be very discreet in order to get images.

At 6 a.m. on our second morning the police were attacked with a grenade. We arrived at the station just as they brought in the wounded. Around 9 p.m. we heard another grenade explode, I grabbed my body-armour and cameras. Garry and I ran towards the police station where a wounded officer was brought in. While I was photographing him we heard a burst of automatic gunfire so we immediately took off in the direction of the shooting.

Running down the street in pitch dark another long burst tore through the air. As we dived into hard cover I stumbled and crashed headlong into a metal doorway cracking my head in two places. As I hit the ground the flashgun ripped from my camera rendering it useless.

Another explosion ripped through the air and a longer gun battle started.

Back at the station the police were loading up with ammunition and blacking out their faces in preparation for further combat. We hung around for awhile but as it seemed quiet we returned to the hotel via the deserted plaza little knowing it would become the scene of a pitched battle minutes later.

We had just sat down on the steps of the hotel and opened a beer when gunfire erupted at the very next corner. We scrambled for cover as the firing intensified. Unseen gunmen opened up on the police and they somewhat blindly fired back.

There was about 90 minutes to two hours of pretty intense fighting, all of which was impossible to photograph because of the darkness. We were also unable to pinpoint exactly who was where or who was shooting in which direction. For the quality of pictures we could make it was not worth exposing ourselves to the heavy gunfire. Once I had sunk a few more beers and stripped off my very sweaty body armour I slept like a log.

13th February

Over the past few days we had been trying to set up a meeting with the ELN rebels who had kidnapped my friend Scott Dalton and his companion Ruth Morris. Our local fixer had made contact and had arranged for us to be collected then handed to someone else and driven out of town. We could expect to be moved around possibly for a couple of days until the rebels were happy it was not a trap, then they would meet with us.

However these are tough times and although Scott and Ruth were released, the ELN are not the only group taking hostages at this point. We faced a difficult decision but in the end we had too many doubts about our safety and so had to bail on that plan.

I still have a couple of weeks left but it feels as though I have been here months already. It's been exhausting but I do feel as though I am making very good use of my time. Certainly this week in Saravena has provided a lot of new material and experiences.

Bogotá - On Friday evening whilst still in Saravena, we saw the news of the huge explosion in Bogotá. It turned out to be the worst urban terror attack in Colombia for 10 years. An up market club called El Norgal had been destroyed by a massive car bomb leaving 33 dead and 174 wounded. Accusations are flying in all directions but the FARC seem to have more fingers pointed at them than anybody else.

On Saturday we flew back to Bogotá, since when all flights have been suspended and the rebels have declared an armed strike threatening to burn any vehicles trying to use roads in the area.

Tomorrow I will fly down to Puerto Asís on the border with Ecuador.

There was a big battle in this area last week between the FARC and the paramilitaries resulting in about 50 deaths. The residents of several outlying villages have begun heading to larger towns for safety. They are moving into disused schools and being fed by the local Red Cross. I want to document this displacement and hopefully get something more on the paras.

A Government soldier on manoeuvres in Arauca.

Government troops on manoeuvres in Arauca.

A Government soldier helps a companion into a truck at the end of manoeuvres in Arauca.

US Green Beret Special Forces train Government troops in counter insurgency
techniques as part of an effort to protect oil pipelines in the region.
Saravena, Arauca.

A female Government soldier puts camouflage paint on a child's face during
a "hearts and minds" operation aimed at improving the image of the military
and gathering intelligence.
Saravena, Arauca.

Naval forces use heavily armed
'Piranha' speedboats to patrol
a river used by both rebel and
paramilitary groups to transport
weapons and drugs.
Rio Atrato, Chocó.

US assistance in the form of Blackhawk helicopter gunships and troop carriers take off from a forward operating base. Tame, Arauca.

A symbolic graveyard bears witness to the human
cost to the Military forces for their part in Colombia's
power struggle.
Tame, Arauca.

Putumayo

19th February

Puerto Asís - The first thing I saw upon leaving the airport was a procession of local children and their parents pushing the coffin of their teacher towards the cemetery. She had been gunned down in front of her class the previous day.

I found it a very moving experience watching the school children and the teacher's family walking though the streets. They held hands in the church as they sang hymns. Outside government soldiers stood guard against a further attack. Later at the graveside the coffin was opened so the teacher's daughters could say a final goodbye. I struggled to imagine how life continues in a town where random assassinations have become a daily occurrence.

From Puerto Asís I headed directly to La Hormiga to photograph the families who had been displaced by fighting in the villages of El Tigre and El Placer. I also made contact with the local commander of the paramilitaries. I explained to him my desire to photograph AUC troops in the field. He agreed to take me next morning to meet a large group of his fighters in the surrounding countryside.

Next day we set off in a pick-up truck and passed through several military check-points making a complete farce of the Government's claim to be fighting both the AUC and FARC. The heavily armed group was waved through without problem.

We reached a small hamlet near La Dorada where 300 to 400 AUC fighters were camped. I was greeted by one of the commanders who remembered me from the year before when I passed through El Tigre.

I photographed the troops formed up on parade and then at rest. They prepared a meal and proudly showed me their weapons and home-made Claymore anti-personnel mines.

Back in Puerto Asís I decided to spend sometime with the same family I lived with last year. I was in for some disturbing surprises. Last year when I met Marylin on the bus she had been buying clothes in the city and selling them here in her town.

She now admitted to me that she had joined the AUC and had been active in combat in El Tigre. Another female friend who had been fighting at her side had been killed along with 25 other paras and at least 15 rebels. When the combat ceased the entire population of the village fled.

Her brother is working on a coca plantation and carries a pistol which he sleeps with under his pillow. Last year I was living with what seemed like a normal family. This year in the same house with the same people, I was living with active paramilitaries - a strange and unsettling experience.

I did not however find it particularly shocking, this is after all a country torn apart by every type of violence. Military, paramilitary, FARC, coca farmer all different sides of the same dice. Only luck, or lack of it depending on your perspective, dictates which side you are on.

Townsfolk and family at the graveside of a school teacher murdered in front of her class. Puerto Asís, Putumayo

A displaced woman searches for
her children at a Red Cross food
and clothing distribution center.
La Hormiga, Putumayo.

Families displaced by fighting begin to build new homes.
Mocoa, Putumayo.

A young girl watches as her father works on constructing a new house for the family.
Mocoa, Putumayo.

Guahibo Indians who survived an alleged paramilitary massacre in Betoyes living in a disused school. Saravena, Arauca.

A Guahibo Indian mother and child displaced by military and paramilitary action in Betoyes. Saravena, Arauca. »

AUC paramilitary fighter.
La Dorada, Putumayo.

An AUC explosives specialist displays a homemade Claymore anti personnel mine. La Dorada, Putumayo.

«Paramilitary fighters parade for inspection by their regional commander. La Dorada, Putumayo.

An old man crosses the plaza of a town controlled by paramilitary forces but surrounded by the FARC. La Dorada, Putumayo.

Previous page: A young passenger glances around anxiously as her bus approaches a checkpoint. Puerto Asís, Putumayo.

Welcome to Saravena

13th June

Saravena - Welcome to Sarajevo more like! This is the most attacked town in Colombia. When I was last here 3 months ago the streets crackled nightly with automatic gunfire as the police traded shots with snipers from the local urban militia groups. The gunfire was punctuated by the 'whumph' of grenades exploding.

Even from the aircraft door with the ruined airport buildings in view we noticed a different vibe. There was no movement on the road beyond. No cabs waited to transport the arriving passengers into town, just the heavily armed police and soldiers. They made us sign a waiver in which we agreed to abide by the curfew and not to leave the town limits.

Outside the airport a silver pick-up truck backed away from the curb, I waved the driver down and begged a ride into town. During the journey he explained that the rebels had ordered a strike. No shops or businesses were allowed to open and no transportation was permitted to operate. The penalty for breaking this strike was left unspoken but understood.

We passed through deserted streets lined with shuttered shops and restaurants. There was plenty of room at the hotel as no one else was in town. A few hours before we arrived a rebel had blown himself to pieces while activating a motorcycle bomb. The rebels had used explosives to destroy three electrical pylons leaving the town without any power.

We dropped our backpacks in the dingy rooms. Shouldering our cameras and bullet-proof vests we then strolled down to the fortress-like police station. We passed the bombed-out ruins of the mayor's office and local businesses unlucky enough to have been hit by the rebels' highly inaccurate and incredibly destructive 'cylindros' - domestic gas canisters packed with high explosives and shrapnel.

The police were all smiles and handshakes. At least one recognised me from another time and place. The slab of photos I carry from previous visits were enthusiastically passed from person to person. They arrived bent and fingerprinted to the Captain who began arranging photo layouts on his desk while calling for coffee or cold drinks to be brought for his guests.

Over the next few days we became good friends with many of the 180 police officers fighting to keep a grip on the few blocks around their besieged station.

The relationship between the Captain and his men was interesting to witness. He stood bouncing a basket ball as he reminded them of the dangers they faced out on the streets. They strapped on their helmets and body-armour and double-checked their weapons before setting off on two hour patrols that passed through the most dangerous barrios in Saravena. We accompanied several of these patrols at different times of day, but evening time was the most tense.

Snipers or grenade throwers potentially lurked in every shadow. Each approaching car spelt the possibility of an attack. Bicycles and motorcycles parked by the roadside caused extra beads of sweat to trickle down our necks as we criss-crossed from one side of the road to the other to give them as wide a berth as possible. Whether those additional few meters would make any difference if they exploded spraying shrapnel in every direction we could only guess.

When the patrol halted to search passers-by at road junctions there did not appear to be any safe place to stand. My heart seemed to thud against the ceramic plate in my body armour. Every muscle was tense and I was ready to dive for cover. Eyes undoubtedly following our every move, maybe peering down the barrel of a gun and waiting for a chance to cut us down in deadly crossfire.

Arriving back at our hotel with the false sense of security it offered us always caused a release of long held breath. Lighting a cigarette, opening a warm beer, complaining about the warm beer and lack of action on the patrol became a cycle, repeated over and over. Would the attack everyone was anticipating come during the night? Would those 'cylindros' come crashing into our hotel? Maybe, but probably not! Another few beers and more cigarettes helped to pass the time.

One morning I walked down to the river with Eros, my photographer friend from California, who I had worked with in the south a year before.

From the bridge we could see a crowd of women and children washing their clothes at the water's edge. These were a few of the hundreds of Indians displaced by paramilitary action in a town some 80 kilometers away. Their desperate flight from their homes had left them exhausted and frightened.

We moved towards them slowly, crouching in order to appear less of a threat, smiling until our faces hurt. Eight-year-old girls in tattered dresses hugged naked, crying babies closer to their chests, their eyes darting around trying to assess the danger. Our smiles were not returned, clothes and dirty children were hurriedly scrubbed. Wet clothes were stuffed into bags, the tiny babies strapped onto mothers' backs and without a backward glance the refugees climbed the steep riverbank and returned to the smoky, filthy, camps into which we were not allowed to follow.

The pattern of our days was broken only by the arrival of another friend Hector, also a veteran of this conflict. The first pictures he made in Saravena were of a dead Indian, killed in a drunken fight by machete blows to the head. The body was dumped as if in sick humour in a disabled only parking area in front of the police station.

As the police examined the body and we snapped away, the stories of rebels filling corpses with explosives making us nervous.

Due to the lack of transport the police offered to take us anywhere we needed to go. Wanting access to the military base we asked to go there. We climbed into the back of a small saloon car with a driver and police officer riding shotgun. Six more men on three motorcycles gunned their engines, while eight more scrambled aboard a pickup truck. The convoy shot away from the police station, skidding around corners with tyres scrabbling for purchase and scattering cyclists at every blast of the horn.

This bit of excitement was available anytime we requested it and we soon learned that the getting thrown around in the back of the pick-up was much more fun, offered better photo opportunities and in the event of an ambush, would be easier to exit.

Given the difficulties of working in Saravena with the lack of transport etc. we decided to pull out. All that roaring around with the police is no way to keep a low profile. Although it's certain the town will witness another vicious attack very soon the security forces are poised to retaliate hard and fast and so the rebels are biding their time.

That attack would probably produce great images but the tension we were feeling and the lack of other angles to pursue made us feel that a change of location would be more productive.

A police officer stands guard in a fortified bunker at a road junction.
Saravena, Arauca.

Police officers keep fit in an improvised gym in their besieged compound.
Saravena, Arauca.

A patrol passes graffiti by the rebel group ELN who as well as the paramilitaries
and FARC are fighting for control of the town.
Saravena, Arauca.

A police patrol searches a group of men for weapons. Saravena, Arauca.

Following page: Due to the risk from snipers and booby trapped vehicles or objects the police conduct
all patrols on foot and well spread out to increase their survivability if attacked. Saravena, Arauca.

Evening and night patrols are the most dangerous and the police take no chances; stopping and searching anyone outside after curfew. Saravena, Arauca.

The body of an Guahibo Indian killed during and argument is examined outside the police station.
Saravena, Arauca.

Weapons maintenance is crucial in a place where a stoppage could prove fatal.
Saravena, Arauca.

A young girl rides past a police patrol as she hurries to get home before curfew. Saravena, Arauca.

Holy Communion.
Saravena, Arauca.

A victim of assassination is mourned by his family.
Saravena, Arauca.

In Purgatory

19th July

Puerto Asís - The first explosion broke my recent grip on sleep. Unsure if it was only a door slamming somewhere in the hotel I lay still, listening. Two more explosions, moments apart and a scream from the street had me on my feet pulling on clothes and lacing boots.

Outside the street was quiet and very dark. As my eyes adjusted I could see townspeople peering from doorways. They couldn't tell me what had happened, or where, but there had been three explosions and they sounded close. I picked my way through the shadows in the direction of the military post in the centre of town. The soldiers were standing casually in the street which meant the explosions had occurred further away than I believed. These men were not expecting an attack. They said the bombs or grenades had gone off on the edge of town but couldn't guess what the target had been.

Back in my room with body-armour and camera-bag within arm's reach and rucksack packed ready to evacuate at a moment's notice I lay thinking about the last three weeks here in Putumayo. Over the last 21 days I spent too much time waiting for contacts that never arrived, following false and expensive leads and questioning my justifications for being here.

My companions and I had travelled deeper into paramilitary country where we had previously worked and knew local commanders. The situation in these small towns locked down by paramilitary control was tense. FARC rebels were circling in the surrounding countryside waiting for an opportunity to claw back some territory. Therefore the paramilitaries did not feel it was safe to take us out to where their troops were massed. Disappointed we headed back to Puerto Asís only to be frustrated further by the news that we had missed an opportunity to photograph the coca being harvested by a mere few hours.

In paramilitary country once more, but this time alone, I again sought permission to visit their camps. The explosions of the other night firmly put a stop to that possibility. They suggested I try again in a few weeks. I hitched a ride back from the Ecuadorian border with a paramilitary commander. He was driving a jeep that he told me was given to his group by one of the big oil companies in exchange for helping to protect their interests in the region. Torrential rain and a dreadful road surface made the drive treacherous.

The commander, who was unarmed, told me he was unknown to the FARC in this area. The FARC fronts that operate here have a vicious reputation and meeting them in his company could have had fatal consequences for both of us. He told me whenever we were passing through areas of increased danger, but the roadblocks never materialized. Eventually we reached a junction where he dropped me to await onward transport. After shaking my hand firmly and wishing me luck he accelerated away into the pouring rain.

A year on since our first meeting on the bus I arrived at Marylin's home in a battered taxi, I sat and drank an ice cold beer with her father whilst waiting for her to return from an 'errand'. I then walked hand-in-hand with her and her four-year-old daughter Natalie down the rutted cart track to a tree shaded swimming hole in the river behind here house. With her daughter splashing around near the river bank we drifted in each others arms into the deeper, cooler water. I felt there was a change in the atmosphere, I couldn't put my finger on exactly what I was sensing. I asked her if thing's would be different between us if I stayed at a hotel in the town rather than with her family. She agreed that it might make it easier for us to be together. That evening she arrived for dinner, we ate in the balcony restaurant of the hotel.

As we shared a bottle of wine and listened to the chorus of insects that go into overdrive the moment the sun disappears I began to think that the year of ground work I had put in was about to pay off. Marylin did stay the night. And next morning she decided to tell me her secret...

Puerto Asis, Marylin's home town sits just a degree or two above the equator. Air conditioning was an expensive extra and I was broke. The tiny hotel room was stifling, and as we lay curled amongst the sweat soaked sheets, with the shouts of street vendors and the roar and fumes of the early morning traffic drifting in though our balcony windows, Marylin said she had 'something' to tell me. She then hit me with a confession that would both thrill and confuse me. She explained that in the months that I had been away in Iraq her role within the AUC had changed, she had joined the urban militia and become an assassin. Her job was now to eliminate informers and traitors. At this point, she told me, she had killed at least 10 people in the area.

I lit a cigarette and inhaled deeply, Marylin looked at me through the smoke as I exhaled, waiting to see how I would respond to what she had just told me. Strangely, her confession did not have the impact one would expect, I did not recoil in horror. The months I had spent in both Colombia and in Iraq surrounded by violence had altered my perspective. I don't think that I had become immune to death or pain and suffering but I had certainly become less easily shocked and had begun particularly in Colombia to realise that in some way everyone had a part in this culture of violence that lurked in every shadow of every town I visited. The difference between victim and victor, rebel and refugee, assassin and activist seemed often to be only a matter of perspective.

I had always enjoyed the company of the 'doers', the rebels and the soldiers who were out risking their lives for causes I supposed they believed in. I was left cold by those wealthy, well dressed beauty queens who inhabited the upmarket dance clubs of Bogotá and knew nothing of the reality of what occurred outside their world of privileged insulation.

Although I would later feel very differently, my initial reaction to Marylin's words were an acceptance that may have bordered on approval. I guess I felt that as war zone lovers go she was pretty 'cool'.

In the beginning her visits to my hotel room often armed with a pistol did not disturb me greatly. At first I don't think the real implications of what Marylin was doing had filtered through the surreal haze. I was young and living out a great adventure. This was surely the closest I would ever get to someone who was truly and totally involved and immersed in this conflict.

The woman I had only recently begun sleeping with was a hired killer and there was a gun on my bedside table. Watching her take the pistol from her belt, unbutton her jeans and slip into bed I somehow couldn't quite equate the woman in my arms with the bodies I had seen in the local morgue, their heads shattered by gunshots at close range. Murders that her claims indicated she may have committed. High on a combination of the heady tropical climate, local rum and in the arms of a beautiful 22 year old, fantasy and reality became blurred. It felt like I was living in a Quentin Tarantino movie.

After a few weeks my mind was in turmoil over my relationship with Marylin. One morning Marylin told me that the previous night she had persuaded a friend to help her decapitate and dismember a woman she had been contracted to kill. This was no informer but, rather, a friend of hers had paid her to kill her boyfriend's other girlfriend. She described so graphically what had happened, with so little feeling that at last reality kicked in. I found my feelings about her changing and madly accelerating towards a point of no return.

Had her 'profession' not been independently confirmed by a local trustworthy source I might have been able to write-off her story as the creations of a bored and imaginative 22-year-old girl living in the modern day equivalent of the Wild West. The romantic light that I had been viewing her in was fading fast. She no longer seemed to be a legitimate part of a civil conflict but had evolved into a freelance killer, taking life in exchange for money, no more no less.

Although I still found her sexually attractive and wanted to be with her, something else was ricocheting around in my brain. Maybe some of the thoughts that would have occurred to anyone else much earlier were at last beginning to filter through.

Over the past year I had photographed her swimming in the river with her daughter and reading bedtime stories. But now the images I was recording concentrated almost entirely on the other side of her life. I was, maybe with some thoughts of self preservation in mind, reducing her to being a 'subject'.

Marylin washes clothes whilst her nephew, niece and daughter play in the river. Puerto Asís, Putumayo.

Following page: Mother and daughter playing in a swimming hole. Puerto Asís, Putumayo.

Marylin reads her nephews and daughter a bedtime story.
Puerto Asís, Putumayo.

Marylin's older brother watches as she cleans her pistol.
Puerto Asís, Putumayo.

Marylin strips and cleans a
pistol, her cousin and nephew
are sat nearby.
Puerto Asís, Putumayo.

Marylin's brother removes her pistol that has been left on
the bed where her daughter and cousin are playing.
Puerto Asís, Putumayo.

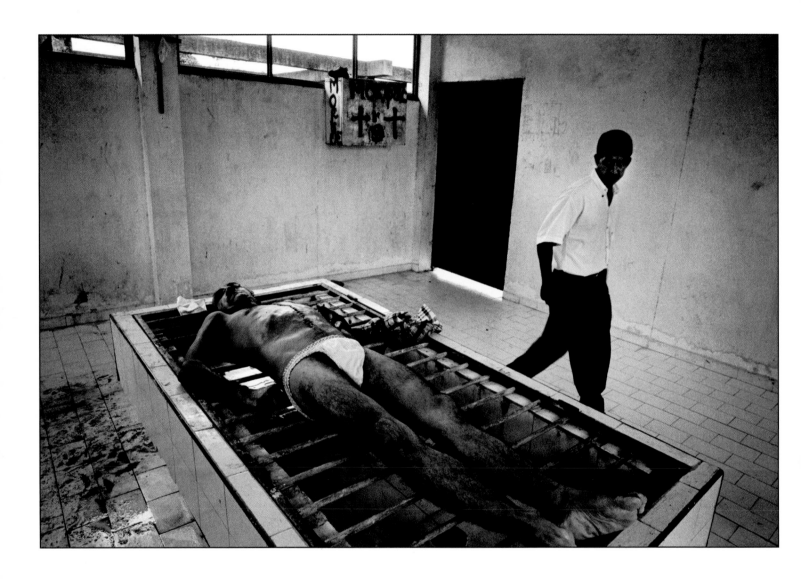

The body of a man with two gunshot wounds to the head lies on a gurney in the town morgue.
Puerto Asís, Putumayo.

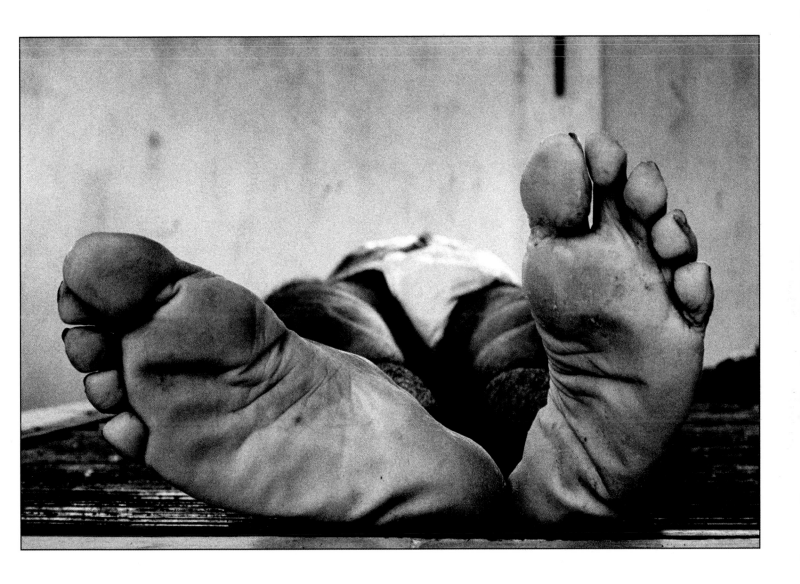

In this highly contested region the morgue is rarely empty as both FARC and paramilitaries murder informers and uncooperative coca farmers.
Puerto Asís, Putumayo.

Return to Caguan

17th August

San Vicente - It is my first time back in what I feel is my favourite town in Colombia in over 18 months. I have a special affection for San Vicente and those who live here. This is where the concept for my project first started to take shape and this region where I have had some of my most intense experiences.

My friends in Bogotá didn't know of any journalists who had been to San Vicente since the end of the peace process. A few had ventured close by road from Florencia but not right back into the old capital of FARC control. Because of this no one was able to tell me if the road was safe to travel or what the chances were of running into a hostile FARC checkpoint. Having promised myself that I would one day return to see how life had changed I decided to take the gamble.

The Satena flight from Bogotá deposited me in the rainswept capital of the department Florencia. I found a collectivo taxi making the 150km run out to San Vicente. The journey was tense but rewarding. To drive past the site of the bus bomb and then an hour or so later after crossing Rio Puerto Rico by ferry raft to pass the place I experienced my first combat was unsettling.

I thought of how much more I had seen since then and how my ideas about Colombia had changed. A lot had changed for me but for the people who live in the towns along this highway the last 18 months had brought few changes for the good. The FARC were no longer walking the streets but had been replaced by Government troops and paramilitaries. The reports of bombs and assassinations that reached the news suggested this had not made it any safer for the locals.

Being back in San Vicente after so long was a joy, the look on the faces of old acquaintances who I am sure never expected to see me again was all the reward I needed for making the trip.

The town had certainly altered; the street in which I lived for a while was now a fifty meter wide crater. A bomb had demolished several homes and the local Government office. It was detonated by the FARC to celebrate their 39th anniversary. I also met the local gravedigger who had buried more than 100 assassination victims since the peace talks broke down.

The rebels who I was both excited and fearful about meeting again were nowhere to be seen. My enthusiasm about tracking them down had been dampened by repeated warnings not to go anywhere near them. The locals I knew confirmed that any contact with the FARC in this region was both difficult and very dangerous. Suddenly all the frustrations, setbacks and disappointments of this trip came crashing on top of me and I felt that the chances of producing anything more from this trip were unlikely.

I decided to ask Marylin if she would be prepared to let me interview her about her life and what she had become involved in. Wearing a balaclava and brandishing a pistol she permitted me to video our conversation.

I began by asking her how she had first become involved with the paramilitaries and why she decided to join them. How she had been persuaded to kill her first victim and how she felt about it; whether it had become easier with time. What did she believe her role was in Colombia's conflict and what were her feelings about the future.

She told me:
When I killed the first person, I was afraid, I was scared. I killed the first person just to see if I could. But there is an obligation to kill. If you don't, they kill you. That's why the first was very hard, because the person I killed was kneeling down begging not to be killed. The person was crying, saying, "Don't kill me. I have children." That's why it was difficult and sad. If you don't kill that person, someone else from the AUC will come to kill you.

So in that case, you must kill to not be killed. After the killing you keep trembling. You can't eat or talk to anyone. I was at home, but I kept imagining the person begging not to be killed. I shut myself inside, but with time I forgot everything. The superiors always say, "Don't worry, that was just the first time. When you kill the second one, it will all be O.K." But you keep trembling.

The second time is only a bit easier, but as they say here, "If you can kill one, you can kill many more." You have to lose the fear. Now I am still killing and nothing happens. I feel normal. Before I had an obligation to kill, I was sent to kill. But once I left the organisation I was not obligated. I only do the job for money. Now I get paid per job. With them I was paid monthly; it didn't matter how many I killed. But now when I do a job, I get paid cash. It doesn't matter what the problem is. When they pay me and tell me to kill, that's what I do.

Yes [I killed one of my friends], because in one situation they were going to kill me. They told me to take care because they worked for the other side and had connections with the guerrillas. And so it was my life or theirs. So I asked permission to do it, which [the AUC] gave me. [The AUC] investigated and it came out positive that [my friends] worked for the guerrillas, so I killed them. It was very painful for me [to kill one friend]. I was at the burial and at the vigil. It hurt me to see his mother crying, knowing I was the one guilty of having caused that. That was very painful. But it's your life and you're taught in the [AUC] school: First you, then the others.

More than anything, the fight here is for money and that comes from coca. The group with the most money and people will be the strongest. The AUC is financed by coca and so is the FARC. As a result, there is fighting to take over towns and to control the people and the money. There is lots of combat and many deaths. That's the motive—coca and money. In total, I have killed 23 people with my own hands.

An incredible sadness washed over me as I listened to this intelligent and attractive young woman who I had known for a long time and had become close to, talk of her life.

I sat looking at this young woman who I felt was an extreme victim of circumstance. Her boredom and quest for excitement had brought her into contact with the paramilitaries who, in expert manner, built on many years experience, had brainwashed her and left her with no respect for human life. Not her own, nor her family's, and certainly not those whose lives she snuffs out.

I was becoming sick of looking at and talking to her; her excuses, or rather lack of them, riled me and I told her that for me she represented everything that was wrong with this country. Her experiences helped me to understand how the armed groups attract so many recruits. That boredom, greed, lack of prospects and a desensitisation to the suffering of others are prime requirements for participating in this dreadful catastrophe.

From my privileged and ultimately unqualified position as an outsider I found it impossible to identify with her, only to be angry, upset and judgemental. Reducing her to a 'subject' had not worked, I did not seem able to be detached and objective or able to put my own feelings aside. I had travelled too far beyond that point. Whilst on one level I relished the intensity of what I was experiencing there was a price to be paid for getting in so deep and it was costly and painful. I realised that the things I had seen and heard in the last couple of months were incredible. Through them my passion for Colombia had grown and my understanding of what was happening in this much misunderstood country had broadened. But I felt that I had lost something and been damaged by the experiences too.

I had been feeling that if I returned in the future to find that Marylin had been killed it would be a traumatic experience. I now began to believe that I would certainly be sad for her family but not for Marylin herself. She had chosen to live by the sword so to speak, inevitably, given time, this meant she would surely die by it.

A prostitute bathes in the river
before going to work in one of
the towns many brothels.
San Vicente del Caguan, Caquetá.

A young daredevil impresses
onlookers as he leaps from a
suspension bridge into the
Rio Caguan.
San Vicente del Caguan, Caquetá.

Children play school whilst Government troops conduct a checkpoint nearby.
Puerto Asís, Putumayo

Largely ignored by the Government, those disabled either by the conflict or accident must continue to seek work to get by.
Florencia, Caquetá.

El Chocó

20th May

Quibdo - The jungles of El Chocó stretch from the Panamanian border down and out to the Pacific coast. I knew little of this region except that it was one of the wettest places on earth. The mainly black inhabitants of Chocó make up a huge percentage of the overall population and that there are several indigenous tribes living in the jungle too.

It was in Bellavista in May 2002 that the worse massacre in the recent history of Colombia had occurred. The FARC and paramilitaries were fighting all around the town. The fighting was so heavy that many townsfolk were hiding in the church. The paras apparently set up some kind of position close to the church and when the FARC attacked with their dreadfully inaccurate homemade mortars they missed the position and hit the church killing 119; mainly women and children.

This was also the area where a British backpacker I had met at the Platypus hostel in Bogotá had died in a firefight between rebels and Government soldiers. The rebels had pulled him off a night bus he was unwisely taking from Meddellin to Quibdo.

The conflict is still raging in the area as the rebel groups and paramilitaries seek to gain control of the land. In El Chocó the cash crop is not coca as elsewhere but African Palm. The palm oil is used for all sorts of products and is big business. It illustrates how those that blame this whole conflict on drugs are quite wrong. This conflict is about greed and power. Where there is no coca the groups are killing each other and innocent civilians for control of whatever is the most valuable commodity. People will always find something to fight over.

El Chocó has a very high rate of displacement caused by this land grabbing. Bellavista is now home to at least 1200 persons displaced from surrounding villages.

Quibdo the capital of the region is a short flight from Bogotá. From the air I got a real sense of entering a Colombia I had never before seen. The ugly looking city squats on the banks of the Rio Atrato. The area had been hit by extreme weather in the past and also a large fire that had forced 800 already displaced persons out of their temporary shelter. Being ignored by central Government hasn't helped much with the rebuilding.

Only a few streets in the centre were tarmac, the side streets little more than mud and the houses on either side were hovels of wood and tin. The Afro-Colombians who populate this area struck me immediately as very friendly and more prone to cracking a smile and laughing out loud than the people in other parts of the country.

Quibdo to Bellavista was a five hour trip along the river by speedboat. It was an early start and a mob had gathered as they do near any bus, boat or donkey in Colombia to fight over tickets and seats. The reason for Chocó being known as one of the wettest places on earth became clearly apparent. The heavens opened and all of a sudden five hours crammed into a floating death trap careering along the jungle waterways began to look a little less romantic.

I left the squabbling horde and took a few minutes to purchase a sturdy looking umbrella and a bag of food for the journey. The fist sized balls of potato and meat wrapped in some kind of batter are a delicious Colombian speciality and a good staple for any journey. I rationed myself to just a couple of tinto's; the tiny cups of sweet black coffee that have the kick of jet fuel. Toilet stops would be few and far between and the journey looked like it might be uncomfortable enough without having a full bladder.

The hours slipped by. The boat stopped a few times at riverside checkpoints. I was a little nervous each time the boat slowed not sure how either the rebels or paramilitaries would view my presence here. Fortunately it was Government forces each time. They checked my papers along with everyone else and waved us on.

Bellavista was not the kind of place to have a hotel but I found a room in a family house. It turned out to be one of the most unpleasant places I have ever stayed. The town had little in the way of power or running water. The shower was a bucket of water to be tipped over ones head whilst standing next to the kitchen. There was a real sit down toilet but that too need flushing with the water bucket.

The bedding stank of old sweat. The humidity knocked me sideways. I spent a lot of time fending off various flying bloodsuckers that come with the territory. All in all I was enjoying myself though. Conveniently there was a liquor store close by and a bottle of rum helped dull my sense of smell and forget about the insect bites.

At first light each day I walked along the river to Nuevo Bellavista where the displaced had built their new homes. Life starts early so there were always folks gathering water or wood. The fishermen would be out and children were playing in the dirt. It only took about thirty minutes to stroll the length of the settlement, nodding hello to people and stopping to make a few pictures here and there. In the late afternoon when the light was nice again I repeated my walk. I did this each day and the people became less suspicious and friendlier day by day.

Even the Indians eventually began to return my smiles and I found a few who spoke Spanish. They told me a little about what had been happening in the region.

The paramilitaries were apparently trying to force them out of their village so the land could be used for African Palms. To try and get the people to leave they had put a blockade on the river not allowing anyone who left to carry food from the village to sell at market and not allowing anyone returning to bring in medicine for the sick in the village.

I wanted to see one of these paramilitary river blocks and after some persuasion an Indian agreed to take me to his village. It would be an eight hour trip by dugout canoe and there was no guarantee that the paras would let me pass let alone take pictures. I felt it unlikely they would kill me given how much attention that might draw. They did after all let the Red Cross and other NGO's live and work in the area. But they probably had a way of seeking permission for their trips in country.

I spent a sleepless night worrying about the trip. Finally the decision to proceed or not was taken out of my hands. At first light I went back to the Indian ready to embark on a long paddle only to hear that another villager had arrived in the night with news of heavy fighting near their homes. My guide told me he was going nowhere and that was the end of that.

Just before leaving Bellavista I joined a naval patrol for a couple of hours. By making regular sweeps along the river the navy hoped to disrupt the movement of the illegal armed groups and the weapons and drugs that were trafficked in the area.

I had been warned not to have anything to do with either the police or military until I was ready to leave town. The locals do not trust the Government forces and if they saw me even talking to them my access elsewhere would disappear.

The local paramilitary leader was a well known figure in town. He was pointed out to me as he stood speaking to a senior army officer visiting Bellavista. Despite his being well known and the leader of an illegal militia he was not being interfered with. Locals told me they often saw boatloads of paramilitaries passing by under the very noses of the army, navy and police. They also accused the troops of using some of the displaced women as prostitutes and confiscated drugs as a currency. That could be fiction but it would be no surprise to find out that it was true.

After joining a navy patrol for a few hours I was keen to head back to Bogotá. The river trip back didn't appeal. The heat, humidity and monotony of the place were getting to me. I took a ferry across the river to Vigia del Fuerte and searched out a place to buy a ticket for the three seater Cessna that made daily flights to Quibdo. It cost two and half times the price of the boat ride but took a fraction of the time. It would also give me a different view of the jungle.

There is no airport or runway so the plane lands on the main dirt road that runs through the center of town. After heavy rain, which occurs most days this can be hazardous as the dirt turns to mud. My flight was cancelled the first day due to the weather. I was stuck for another night so I crossed back to my stinking accommodation in Bellavista and another bottle of rum.

Next morning Javier the pilot made it to Vigia. In his uniform of pressed white shirt and dark trousers he would have not looked out of place in the cockpit of a 747. The little Cessna clawed its way into the air and took thirty minutes to cross the breathtaking stretch of jungle. Back in Quibdo a group of extremely officious but very polite police officers took my bags apart item by item and brought me back down to earth with a bump.

Displaced families including the children have to work together to survive after being forced from their villages.
Bellavista, El Chocó

Young children displaced by the
power struggle in the surrounding
jungle collect firewood.
Bellavista, El Chocó.

Two young boys living in a displacement camp
replicate the violence that surrounds them by
playing 'war' with wooden guns.
Bellavista, El Chocó.

As rebel groups and paramilitaries battle for control deep in the jungle many
have fled to the towns along the banks of the Rio Atrato where they feel safer.
Bellavista, El Chocó.

Consequences

28th April

Bogotá - Over the course of a year Marylin and I exchanged e-mails periodically. They mainly involved her asking where I was and telling me not to forget her. She told me that things I had said to her after her interview had had a big impact. No one had spoken to her like that, really questioned her about what she was doing with her life. She told me that she did want to make a new beginning but that she knew the AUC do not let their members leave, at least not alive. After a long period of silence I began to fear something had happened and so returned to Puerto Asis to learn the truth.

It took me some time to pluck up the courage to drive out to her home on the outskirts of Puerto Asís to see if she and her family were still around. I wondered if she had perhaps made the break and left to begin a new life or whether, more likely, her past had caught up with her. Given the dreadful things that I already knew she had been involved in, I was at least somewhat prepared for bad news. What I was not ready for was how confusing it was going to be to receive that news.

Her family showed their normal surprise at finding me at their front door. All my fears were confirmed as her father, his eyes welling with tears, told me that Marylin was dead and her brother was bed-bound with paralysis.

She was 25 years and 2 months old when they took her from her home and stoned her to death. They crushed her head with rocks and then shot her.

The next morning her six-year-old daughter Natalie awoke as an orphan, her parents to the loss of a third daughter and her brother so overcome with grief he was unable to walk, talk, or even feed himself.

Marylin was not killed by some local seeking revenge for one of the many deaths that had occurred at her hands during her time as an assassin for the paramilitaries. She was murdered by her own group in a symbolic stoning for being a 'sapo' (literally 'frog' in Spanish) which is what Colombians call informers. Her most recent boyfriend was a Government soldier, convenient enough when the paramilitaries and the Military were working side-by-side in their war to wrestle control of the coca fields of Putumayo from the FARC, but enough to get her killed when that relationship soured and her pillow talk continued.

Marylin's death had a special significance for me, because I too shared some of that pillow talk. We had been friends for more than 2 years and, briefly, lovers. Our lives never had much in common; except that Colombia's dirty little war had both of us locked into its potentially fatal grip.

I found it difficult to speak, I wasn't quite sure what I was feeling or how I should be feeling.

Was I feeling sorry that a young woman who had deliberately taken the lives of other human beings, had received the same kind of street-corner justice she had been responsible for handing out? Was I remembering the conversations we had about changing her life and the e-mails I received from her thanking me and saying she needed to talk more about how she could get out of the mess she was in. Was I wishing I had done more to help her? Was I feeling sorry for her parents and her beautiful daughter, who one day would want an explanation as to why her mother was killed and, maybe, discover the horrors that occurred while she was a sleeping baby?

Was I remembering what it was like to kiss her in those days before I had any clue she was a killer? Was I trying to imagine, or perhaps trying not to imagine, what she looked like after her head had been destroyed with stones and rocks? In truth I was thinking, feeling and imagining all of these things. At the same time I knew that whatever pain her family was feeling, she had caused this same pain to others, with her knife or gun, many, many times. I asked if the family would show me her grave the next day.

Back in my hotel room I let out the longest of breaths, lit a cigarette and stared at the ceiling fan. The whirling blades churned memories of Iraq, my ex-girlfriend and the recent news of Marylin's death, into one. Early next morning together with Marylin's mother and her daughter Natalie, both wearing their best dresses and carrying flowers, I went to see where her body had been laid to rest. The number of bodies demanding burial long ago outstripped the space available.

Marylin's coffin was in a concrete box, built atop the tomb of her sister who also died because of her involvement in the conflict. Alongside lay a much smaller tomb; the remains of another of her sisters. She died of natural causes aged three months. I could not imagine how Marylin's mother felt holding the hand of her granddaughter, looking over the graves of her three daughters.

My hopes of travelling deeper into Putumayo, to photograph paramilitaries, no longer seemed such a good idea. Marylin had always been able to point me in the right direction and warn me when pushing further was not a good idea. I wanted to learn more about her life and death, but didn't want to get killed for asking the wrong questions of the wrong people.

Over dinner and against a background of revving motorbikes and honking trucks another local told me more of what had happen to Marylin, I struggled to understand her fast, quiet Spanish.

I discovered I did not know as much about her life as I thought; she had told me a lot, but kept much back. Between mouthfuls of soup, the woman told me that Marylin had been involved with the AUC for a lot longer than she had admitted to me and that it was commonly believed in the town that she was involved in the massacre of 26 villagers in El Tigre, many of the victims were decapitated and disembowelled before being thrown into a river.

I needed to leave. I booked a seat on the next available flight. As I watched Puerto Asís disappear below me the plane was enveloped by cloud. My thoughts were still with Marylin. I wondered if her story could ever have ended any differently. Was she in fact killed because she was an informer or because, instead, as she indicated in her e-mails, she did really want to leave the AUC and start a new life? This is perhaps what I wanted to believe, that she had a change of heart and wasn't the cold, evil killer she appeared to be.

I doubt I will ever learn the whole truth. Marylin, like the people she herself killed had simply become another casualty in a forgotten dirty war.

Marylin's daughter stands by her tomb.
Puerto Asís, Putumayo.

Afterword

In Colombia two worlds exist. One is of beauty and privilege. It is inhabited by the classes who enjoy a healthy income and a sense of security. It is a bright world of modern cities, beaches, carnivals, restaurants and night clubs. Another world coexists, a world in shadow inhabited by the campasinos, displaced and combatants; one of poverty, violence, fear, repression and invisibility.

'Between the Lines' concentrates attention on this much ignored and often hidden side of Colombian life.

The Colombians living in the shadows lack many things including being identified as individuals, they have largely been reduced to statistics. 'Between the Lines' is an attempt to look into that world in the shade and to examine the impact that decades of war has had on those living there. It is also a chance to discover how few differences there actually are between one group and the next. The people in these photographs all have one thing in common; they are all victims of circumstance. Not one of them has failed to experience pain, fear or loss and does not wish for a better life; in this they are all equal.

When I began making the images in this book it was not with a pure, selfless motive to educate others about Colombia. I was neither a journalist nor even a professional photographer at that time. I travelled to San Vicente de Caguan to meet the FARC for my own benefit, as an exciting challenge, for an adventure and to learn how to be a photojournalist.

I certainly got my adventure but I also found that I had fallen in love with Colombia and its wonderfully hospitable and open people. I realised that criticism like analyses is often done from a position and by those far removed and insulated from the blood, sweat and tears of reality. In order to gain any kind of real understanding one has to be on the ground and immersed in the situation.

My initial idea of documenting life with the left wing militias was not going to be sufficient. I could not with a clear conscience tell the story of just one side in such a complicated struggle. I therefore set out to learn about and photograph many different elements to give the broadest range of perspectives possible.

My knowledge grew quickly. The ideas and opinions I had about the groups involved in the conflict were poorly formed and went through radical changes as I met with them and learnt more about each faction. I met people who scared me, who made me feel safe, who made me want to stay and who made me want to leave. I met people who convinced me with words that Colombia has a bright future to look forward to and others who through their actions made me feel that Colombia may never experience real peace.

The extracts from my email journals hopefully add more context to the photographs and explain a little more of my personal experiences. I tried to be candid in my dispatches. I make no pretence; I was extremely naïve when I first set out to Colombia. I made many mistakes and errors of judgement, some of which could have cost me my life had fortune not fallen on my side. Many times I came close to giving up and on occasions believed I had pushed my luck too far. Some of things I witnessed and experienced during my travels shook me and left me exhausted both physically and emotionally. I appreciate however that no matter how many weeks, months or even years I could spend living alongside these people I could never fully identify with them. As a foreigner I had a certain immunity and could make the choice to leave whenever it suited me; luxuries not available to those I was with.

I hope that I have done justice to and repaid in some way all those Colombians who gave of their time, opened up their lives to me.

Jason P. Howe
London, England. 2008